A step-by-step guide to become a leader most people look upto

How to become a brave leader not a weak leader

Rachel B. Woods

Copyright © by **Rachel B. Woods** 2024. All rights reserved.

Before this document is duplicated or reproduced in any manner, the publisher's consent must be gained. Therefore, the contents within can neither be stored electronically, transferred, nor kept in a database. Neither in Part nor full can the document be copied, scanned, faxed, or retained without approval from the publisher or creator.

The brave leadership

Table of Content

Chapter 1

Chapter 2

Chapter 3

Chapter 4

Chapter 5

Chapter 6

Chapter 7

Chapter 8

Chapter 9

Chapter 10

Chapter 11

Chapter 12

Chapter 1

Introduction: Redefining Leadership

In today's fast-paced and ever-evolving world, the concept of leadership is ripe for redefinition. Gone are the days when leadership was solely defined by titles, status, and wielding power. Instead, a new paradigm is emerging—one that celebrates the inherent potential in every individual and idea.

Leadership, as we now understand it, transcends organisational hierarchies and extends to anyone willing to take responsibility for nurturing that potential. It's about recognizing the unique gifts and talents within each person and having the courage to cultivate them.

In this journey of redefining leadership, we are guided by the pioneering work of good research and a lot of years spent exploring the dynamics of vulnerability, courage, and human connection. Through research and experiences working with leaders across various sectors, This work sheds light on what it truly means to lead with authenticity and courage.

At the heart of daring leadership lies a fundamental shift in mindset—a shift from a scarcity mentality to one of abundance. Instead of viewing power as finite and hoarding it for personal gain, daring leaders understand that power becomes infinite when shared with others. They embrace vulnerability as a catalyst for growth and innovation, leaning into discomfort rather than shying away from it.

As we embark on this journey of redefining leadership, we are challenged to confront the prevailing culture of fear, uncertainty, and scarcity. In a world where technological advancements threaten to outpace our humanity, the need for empathetic, courageous leaders has never been greater.

Through the pages of this book, we will explore the four skill sets that comprise daring leadership—skills that are not only teachable but also observable and measurable. We will delve into the brave work and tough conversations required to cultivate these skills and transform ourselves into the leaders our world desperately needs.

So, let us dare to lead—not with the false pretence of having all the answers, but with a genuine curiosity to ask the right questions. Let us share our power, embrace vulnerability, and cultivate empathy, connection, and courage. For in doing so, we not only elevate ourselves but also inspire others to rise with us.

Chapter 2

The Heart of Daring Leadership

In the ever-shifting landscape of leadership, one quality remains steadfast: courage. At the heart of daring leadership lies an unwavering commitment to courageously embrace the unknown and navigate the complexities of human interaction with grace and authenticity.

Daring leaders understand that true leadership is not about wielding power or asserting authority; it's about recognizing the inherent potential in every individual and having the courage to nurture it. It's about creating an environment where people feel seen, heard, and valued—a place where innovation thrives and collaboration flourishes.

But what does it mean to be courageous in the context of leadership? It means having the courage to challenge the status quo, to ask difficult questions, and to confront uncomfortable truths. It means being willing to take risks and make bold decisions, even in the face of uncertainty.

Courageous leaders also understand the importance of vulnerability. They know that vulnerability is not a weakness but a strength—a gateway to deeper connections and more meaningful relationships. By embracing vulnerability, daring leaders create a culture of trust and authenticity where people feel safe to express their true selves.

In a world that often values strength and stoicism above all else, daring leaders stand out by their willingness to show vulnerability and authenticity. They lead with their hearts as well as their minds, inspiring others to do the same.

But courage alone is not enough. Daring leadership also requires empathy, compassion, and a genuine desire to connect with others on a human level. It's about understanding that leadership is not a solo endeavour but a collaborative journey—a journey that requires us to lean on each other for support and guidance.

As we embark on this journey of daring leadership, let us remember that courage is not the absence of fear but the willingness to act in spite of it. Let us embrace vulnerability as a source of strength and authenticity, and let us lead with empathy, compassion, and heart. For in doing so, we not only become better leaders but also create a better world for all.

Chapter 3

The Courage to Ask: Cultivating Curiosity

In the realm of daring leadership, one quality reigns supreme: curiosity. It is the insatiable hunger to explore, to question, and to seek understanding that propels leaders forward on their journey of growth and discovery.

But why is curiosity so essential to effective leadership? Because it is through curiosity that we uncover new perspectives, challenge existing assumptions, and unlock innovative solutions to complex problems. Curiosity compels us to look beyond the surface and delve into the depths of possibility, opening doors to creativity and insight.

Daring leaders understand that they do not have all the answers—and they don't pretend to. Instead, they approach every situation with a sense of wonder and curiosity, eager to learn from those around them. They understand that true wisdom lies not in knowledge possessed, but in the willingness to ask questions and explore the unknown.

But cultivating curiosity is not always easy. In a world that often values certainty and efficiency above all else, it can be tempting to stick to what we know and avoid venturing into the realm of the unknown. Yet, it is precisely in those moments of uncertainty that curiosity becomes most valuable, guiding us towards new discoveries and opportunities for growth.

Daring leaders also recognize that curiosity is contagious. By fostering a culture of inquiry and exploration within their teams, they inspire others to embrace curiosity as well. They encourage open dialogue, welcome diverse perspectives, and celebrate the spirit of discovery.

In the face of rapid technological advancements and ever-changing market dynamics, curiosity has never been more crucial. It is the driving force behind innovation, adaptation, and resilience—the key ingredients for success in today's fast-paced world.

So let us dare to ask the tough questions, to challenge the status quo, and to embrace the unknown with open arms. Let us cultivate curiosity not only in ourselves but also in those we lead, for it is through curiosity that we unlock the boundless potential of the human spirit.

Chapter 4

The Power of Sharing: Collaboration Over Hoarding

In the realm of daring leadership, a fundamental shift in mindset is taking place—a shift from hoarding power to sharing it freely and generously. Daring leaders understand that true power is not wielded as a tool of domination but rather as a force for collaboration and collective growth.

But what does it mean to share power in the context of leadership? It means recognizing that no one person has all the answers or possesses all the skills needed for success. It means embracing the diversity of perspectives and talents within a team and empowering each individual to contribute their unique gifts to the collective effort.

The brave leadership

Daring leaders understand that when power is shared, it multiplies rather than diminishes. By fostering an environment of trust and collaboration, they create space for innovation to flourish and for teams to achieve greater heights than they ever thought possible.

But sharing power is not just about delegating tasks or distributing responsibilities—it's about fostering a culture of openness, transparency, and mutual respect. It's about creating an environment where everyone feels valued and empowered to speak up, share their ideas, and contribute to the success of the team.

In a world that often rewards competition and individual achievement, daring leaders stand out by their commitment to collaboration and shared success. They understand that true leadership is not about standing at the top of the hierarchy but about lifting others up and bringing out the best in everyone.

But sharing power requires courage. It requires leaders to let go of their ego, to trust in the abilities of their team members, and to embrace vulnerability. It requires them to be willing to admit when they don't have all the answers and to seek input and feedback from those around them.

As we strive to cultivate daring leadership in ourselves and in others, let us remember the power of sharing. Let us embrace collaboration over hoarding, and let us work together to build a future where everyone has the opportunity to thrive.

Chapter 5

Embracing Vulnerability: Lean Into Discomfort

In the landscape of daring leadership, there exists a powerful paradox: the embrace of vulnerability as a catalyst for growth and innovation. While vulnerability is often associated with weakness or insecurity, daring leaders understand that it is in moments of vulnerability that true strength and authenticity emerge.

But what does it mean to embrace vulnerability in the context of leadership? It means having the courage to show up fully and authentically, even when it feels uncomfortable or risky. It means being willing to acknowledge our fears, insecurities, and imperfections—and to share them openly with others.

Daring leaders understand that vulnerability is not a liability but a superpower—a gateway to deeper connections, stronger relationships, and greater resilience. By embracing vulnerability, they create a culture of trust and authenticity where people feel safe to be themselves and take risks.

But leaning into vulnerability is not always easy. It requires us to confront our fears and insecurities head-on, to step outside of our comfort zones, and to embrace the discomfort that comes with growth and change. It requires us to be willing to take risks and make mistakes, knowing that failure is not a sign of weakness but a natural part of the learning process.

In a world that often values strength and stoicism above all else, daring leaders stand out by their willingness to show vulnerability and authenticity. They lead with their hearts as well as their minds, inspiring others to do the same.

But embracing vulnerability is not just about individual growth—it's also about creating a culture where vulnerability is celebrated and encouraged. It's about fostering an environment where people feel safe to take risks, share their ideas, and speak up about their needs and concerns.

Chapter 6

Building Human-Centric Skills in a Technological World

In an era dominated by rapid technological advancements and digital disruption, the value of human-centric skills has never been more apparent. As machines and artificial intelligence continue to automate tasks and streamline processes, the need for uniquely human qualities such as empathy, creativity, and emotional intelligence becomes increasingly vital.

Daring leaders recognize that while technology can augment our capabilities, it can never fully replicate the depth and complexity of human experience. In a world where algorithms can analyse data and perform calculations with lightning speed, it is our ability to connect with others on a human level that sets us apart.

But what exactly are human-centric skills, and why are they so crucial in today's technological landscape? Human-centric skills encompass a wide range of abilities, including empathy, communication, collaboration, adaptability, and resilience. These skills enable us to navigate the complexities of human interaction, understand the needs and perspectives of others, and foster meaningful relationships built on trust and mutual respect.

In a world where the pace of change is accelerating, human-centric skills are becoming increasingly valuable. As industries evolve and job roles shift, the ability to adapt, learn, and grow becomes essential for success. Daring leaders understand that cultivating these skills within themselves and their teams is not just a nice-to-have—it's a necessity for thriving in an uncertain and rapidly changing world.

But building human-centric skills is not always easy. It requires us to step outside of our comfort zones, challenge our assumptions, and embrace diversity and inclusion. It requires us to be willing to listen, learn, and empathise with others, even when their perspectives differ from our own.

In a world where technology can sometimes feel cold and impersonal, human-centric skills are the antidote—the secret sauce that infuses our interactions with warmth, compassion, and humanity. As we navigate the complexities of the digital age, let us remember the importance of building human-centric skills and let us strive to lead with empathy, connection, and courage in all that we do. For in doing so, we not only elevate ourselves but also create a world where technology serves humanity rather than the other way around.

Chapter 7

Empathy, Connection, Courage: The Uniquely Human Advantage

In the realm of daring leadership, three qualities stand out as the cornerstones of human excellence: empathy, connection, and courage. These qualities are not just desirable—they are essential for navigating the complexities of the human experience and inspiring others to reach their full potential.

Empathy is the ability to comprehend, feel and share the feelings of others. It allows us to put ourselves in someone else's shoes, to see the world through their eyes, and to respond with compassion and understanding. Empathy enables us to forge deep, meaningful connections with others, fostering trust and collaboration in the process.

Connection is the bridge that links us to one another, transcending barriers of distance, culture, and circumstance. It is the bond that unites us as human beings, allowing us to share our joys and sorrows, our triumphs and challenges. Connection enables us to build strong, supportive communities where everyone feels valued and included.

Courage is the fuel that propels us forward in the face of adversity and uncertainty. It is the willingness to take risks, to speak up for what is right, and to stand up for those who cannot stand up for themselves. Courage enables us to confront our fears and overcome obstacles, inspiring others to do the same.

But why are empathy, connection, and courage so crucial in today's world? In a society that often values individual achievement over collective well-being, these qualities serve as a beacon of hope—a reminder of our shared humanity and our capacity for compassion and courage.

The brave leadership

In an increasingly interconnected world, empathy, connection, and courage are more important than ever. They enable us to bridge divides, to build bridges of understanding, and to create a more just and equitable society for all.

As we strive to cultivate daring leadership in ourselves and in others, let us remember the power of empathy, connection, and courage. Let us lead with compassion, forge deep and meaningful connections with others, and have the courage to stand up for what is right. In doing so, we not only become better leaders but also create a brighter, more compassionate world for future generations to inherit.

Chapter 8

The Teachable Skill Sets of Daring Leadership

In the pursuit of daring leadership, there exists a profound realisation: that the skills required to lead courageously are not innate traits bestowed upon a select few, but rather teachable, observable, and measurable abilities that anyone can develop with dedication and practice.

The groundbreaking research has uncovered that daring leadership comprises four distinct skill sets, each essential for navigating the complexities of today's rapidly evolving world. These skill sets provide a roadmap for leaders to cultivate the courage, resilience, and authenticity needed to lead with impact and purpose.

1. Rumbling with Vulnerability: Daring leaders understand that vulnerability is not a weakness, but a strength—a catalyst for meaningful connection and growth. They have the courage to lean into discomfort, to embrace vulnerability as a necessary part of the human experience, and to cultivate a culture where authenticity is valued and celebrated.

2. Living into Our Values: Daring leaders are guided by a clear set of values that serve as their moral compass in times of uncertainty and ambiguity. They have the courage to align their actions with their values, even when it requires difficult choices or sacrifices. By living into their values, they inspire others to do the same, fostering a culture of integrity and accountability.

3. Braving Trust: Daring leaders understand that trust is the foundation of strong, resilient relationships. They have the courage to be vulnerable, to communicate openly and honestly, and to honour their commitments. By braving trust, they create environments where people feel safe to take risks, share their ideas, and collaborate effectively.

4. Learning to Rise: Daring leaders embrace failure as a natural part of the learning process, rather than a reflection of their worth or abilities. They have the courage to learn from setbacks, to adapt and grow in the face of adversity, and to encourage others to do the same. By learning to rise, they cultivate resilience and perseverance, enabling themselves and their teams to thrive in the face of challenges.

As we embark on the journey of developing these teachable skill sets, let us remember that daring leadership is not a destination, but a continuous process of growth and self-discovery. Let us have the courage to embrace vulnerability, to live into our values, to brave trust, and to learn to rise. For in doing so, we not only become better leaders but also create a world where courage, compassion, and authenticity reign supreme.

Chapter 9

Learning and Unlearning: Brave Work for Brave Leaders

In the pursuit of daring leadership, there comes a pivotal moment: the recognition that growth and transformation require both learning and unlearning. Daring leaders understand that to truly embody the qualities of courage, authenticity, and resilience, they must be willing to engage in the brave work of challenging old assumptions, confronting limiting beliefs, and embracing new ways of thinking and being.

Learning and unlearning are two sides of the same coin—the yin and yang of personal and professional development. Learning involves acquiring new knowledge, skills, and perspectives, while unlearning requires letting go of outdated habits, biases, and mindsets that no longer serve us.

But why is unlearning so crucial in the context of daring leadership? Because often, it is our deeply ingrained beliefs and assumptions that hold us back from reaching our full potential. Whether it's the belief that vulnerability is a sign of weakness or the assumption that success is measured solely by external achievements, these outdated notions can hinder our ability to lead with authenticity and courage.

Daring leaders understand that unlearning is not easy. It requires us to confront our own biases and blind spots, to challenge the status quo, and to embrace discomfort and uncertainty. It requires us to be humble enough to admit when we don't have all the answers and courageous enough to seek out new perspectives and ideas.

But the rewards of unlearning are immense. By letting go of old habits and beliefs that no longer serve us, we create space for new insights, growth, and innovation. We become more adaptable, resilient, and open-minded leaders, capable of navigating the complexities of an ever-changing world with grace and confidence.

As we embark on the brave work of learning and unlearning, let us approach it with curiosity, humility, and courage. Let us challenge ourselves to question old assumptions, to embrace discomfort, and to cultivate a mindset of continuous growth and improvement. In doing so, we not only become better leaders but also inspire others to embark on their own journey of brave self-discovery and transformation.

Chapter 10

Choosing Courage: Making the Brave Choice

In the tapestry of daring leadership, one thread stands out as the most vibrant and essential: courage. It is the willingness to take bold action in the face of fear, uncertainty, and adversity that distinguishes truly transformative leaders from the rest. But what does it mean to choose courage, and why is it so crucial in today's world?

Choosing courage is not about the absence of fear, but rather the willingness to act in spite of it. It is about embracing discomfort and uncertainty as inevitable companions on the journey of growth and self-discovery. Daring leaders understand that courage is not a fleeting emotion but a conscious choice—a commitment to showing up with integrity, authenticity, and resilience, even when the path ahead is unclear.

But why is courage so essential in the context of leadership? Because leadership is inherently risky. It requires us to step outside of our comfort zones, to challenge the status quo, and to take calculated risks in pursuit of a greater vision. Without courage, we become stagnant, unwilling to push past our own limitations and embrace the unknown.

Daring leaders also understand that courage is contagious. When we choose courage, we inspire others to do the same. Our actions send a powerful message to those around us—that fear is not an obstacle to be avoided but a catalyst for growth and transformation. By leading with courage, we create a ripple effect of positive change that extends far beyond ourselves.

But choosing courage is not always easy. It requires us to confront our own fears and insecurities, to be vulnerable and authentic in the face of uncertainty, and to persevere in the face of adversity. It requires us to be willing to fail, to learn from our mistakes, and to pick ourselves up and try again.

As we navigate the complexities of leadership in an ever-changing world, let us remember the power of courage. Let us choose courage in every moment, knowing that it is the key to unlocking our true potential and inspiring others to do the same. For in the end, it is not our titles or accomplishments that define us, but the courage with which we face life's challenges and embrace its opportunities.

Chapter 11

Stepping Up: Embracing Brave Leadership

In the grand tapestry of leadership, there exists a call to action—a beckoning for individuals to step up and embrace the mantle of brave leadership. It is a summons to rise above the ordinary, to transcend the confines of the status quo, and to lead with courage, compassion, and conviction.

But what does it mean to step up and embrace brave leadership? It means recognizing that leadership is not reserved for those with titles or positions of authority, but rather a choice that anyone can make—a choice to show up fully, authentically, and with purpose, regardless of circumstance or status.

The brave leadership

Brave leadership is not about seeking recognition or glory, but rather a commitment to serving a higher purpose and making a positive impact in the world. It is about leading with integrity, humility, and empathy, and inspiring others to do the same.

But stepping up and embracing brave leadership requires courage. It requires us to confront our own fears and insecurities, to challenge the status quo, and to stand up for what is right, even when it is difficult or unpopular. It requires us to be willing to take risks, to make tough decisions, and to navigate uncertainty with grace and resilience.

Daring leaders understand that the path to brave leadership is not always easy. It is often fraught with obstacles and setbacks, and requires us to constantly push past our own limitations and grow in the process. But they also understand that the rewards of brave leadership are immeasurable—the satisfaction of knowing that we have made a positive difference in the lives of others, and the fulfilment of living a life of purpose and meaning.

As we embark on the journey of stepping up and embracing brave leadership, let us remember that it is not a destination, but a continuous process of growth and self-discovery. Let us have the courage to lead with authenticity and conviction, and to inspire others to do the same. For in the end, it is our collective courage and commitment to making a difference that will shape the future of our world.

Chapter 12

Conclusion: Being Brave with Purpose

In the last chapter of our journey through brave authority, we arrive at a significant realisation: that genuine administration is not fair around what we do, but around who we are, what we grant the world and how we appear up in the world. It is an acknowledgment that administration is not a title or a position, but a choice—a choice to be courageous, to be true, and to make a positive effect in the lives of others.

As we reflect on the lessons learned and the experiences picked up, we are reminded of the control of boldness, helplessness, and compassion in forming our administration travel. We get it that administration is not a singular endeavour, but a collaborative exertion that requires us to incline on one another for bolster and direction. And we recognize that the most compelling pioneers are those who lead with reason and conviction, motivating others to rise to their most noteworthy potential.

But being courageous with reason is not continuously simple. It requires us to go up against our own fears and uncertainties, to challenge the status quo, and to stand up for what is right, indeed when it is troublesome or disliked. It requires us to be willing to take risks, to make intense choices, and to explore instability with beauty and resilience.

Yet, the rewards of being courageous with reason are limitless. They are found in the fulfilment of knowing that we have made a positive distinction in the lives of others, in the fulfilment of living a life of reason and meaning, and in the bequest we take off for future generations.

As we near this chapter and set out on the following stage of our travel, let us carry with us the lessons learned and the bits of knowledge picked up. Let us proceed to be courageous with reason, to lead with judgement and sympathy, and to motivate others to do the same. For in the conclusion, it is our collective boldness and commitment to making a distinction that will shape the future of our world.

www.ingramcontent.com/pod-product-compliance
Lightning Source LLC
Chambersburg PA
CBHW050250230526
45470CB00005B/2197